One Hen

For my favorite entrepreneur, C.R. Mallory – K.S.M.
For Noah Valentine Flessel – E.F.

ACKNOWLEDGMENTS

Many hands helped to refine this tale. A big thank you to my editor,
Val Wyatt, and the team at Kids Can Press for all their support and
guidance; to Eugenie for illustrations that soar; to Mirjam, Nancy, Frank and
Chuck for sharing their microlending expertise; and to Rory for creative
thinking on outreach. I'm indebted to David Simms for introducing me to
Kwabena Darko and to Beth Houle for keeping the conversation that led to
One Hen alive, across continents and years. To Kwabena and all the Kojos
in our world fighting the war on poverty one hen, sewing machine or
vegetable stand at a time goes my deepest admiration.

CitizenKid™ is a trademark of Kids Can Press Ltd.

First paperback edition 2020

Published in Canada and the U.S. by Kids Can Press Ltd.
25 Dockside Drive, Toronto, ON M5A 0B5

Kids Can Press is a Corus Entertainment Inc. company

www.kidscanpress.com

The artwork in this book was rendered in acrylic.
The text is set in Incognito and Goudy Old Style.

Edited by Valerie Wyatt
Designed by Marie Bartholomew

Printed and bound in Buji, Shenzhen, China, in 5/2022
by WKT Company

CM 08 20 19 18 17 16 15 14
CM PA 20 0 9 8 7 6 5 4 3

LIBRARY AND ARCHIVES CANADA CATALOGUING IN PUBLICATION

Title: One hen : how one small loan made a big difference / written by Katie Smith
Milway ; illustrated by Eugenie Fernandes.

Names: Milway, Katie Smith, 1960- author. | Fernandes, Eugenie, 1943-
illustrator.
Series: CitizenKid.
Description: Series statement: CitizenKid | Reprint. Previously published:
Toronto : Kids Can Press, 2008.
Identifiers: Canadiana 20190095121 | ISBN 9781894786096 (softcover)
Subjects: LCSH: Microfinance — Africa — Juvenile fiction. | LCSH: Africa —
Social conditions — 1960- — Juvenile fiction. | LCSH: Africa — Economic
conditions — 1960 — Juvenile fiction.
Classification: LCC PS8626.I48 O54 2020 | DDC jC813/.6 — dc23

Kids Can Press gratefully acknowledges that the land on which our office is located
is the traditional territory of many nations, including the Mississaugas of the
Credit, the Anishnabeg, the Chippewa, the Haudenosaunee and the Wendat peoples,
and is now home to many diverse First Nations, Inuit and Métis peoples.

We thank the Government of Ontario, through Ontario Creates; the Ontario Arts
Council; the Canada Council for the Arts; and the Government of Canada for sup-
porting our publishing activity.

One Hen

How One Small Loan Made a Big Difference

Written by Katie Smith Milway

Illustrated by Eugenie Fernandes

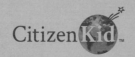

A collection of books that inform
children about the world and inspire
them to be better global citizens

Kids Can Press

This is Kojo.

Kojo tugs the knot tight and hoists a bundle of firewood onto his head. Since his father died, he has had to quit school and help his mother collect wood to sell at the market. It is the last load of the day, and he is tired and hungry.

Kojo and his mother live in a mud-walled house with an open fire for cooking. Beside it is a garden where they grow their own food. They never have much money or much to eat.

As Kojo nears the house, he can smell his mother's *fufu* cooking, their main meal made from cassava and yams. He begins to walk faster.

This is the loan that Kojo gets.

Kojo and his mother live in a village in the Ashanti region of Ghana. None of the twenty families in the village have very much money, but they do have a good idea. Each family promises to save a bit of money so that one family can borrow all the savings to buy something important.

The Achempong family is first to borrow the money. They use it to buy two cartloads of fruit, which they sell for a profit at the market. When they pay back the loan, the Duodu family borrows the money to buy a second-hand sewing machine. They plan to turn the cloth they weave into shirts and dresses to sell.

One day it is Kojo's mother's turn. She uses the loan to buy a cart so she can carry more firewood to market. She also hopes to rent the cart to people who need transport.

There are a few coins left over. Kojo asks if he can have them to buy something for himself. He has a good idea, too.

Kojo's idea is to buy a hen. He and his mother will eat some of the eggs it lays and sell the rest at the market. There is a farmer in a neighboring village with many hens, and Kojo will ask to buy one.

It takes Kojo two hours to walk to the chicken farm. By the time he arrives, he is hot and dusty. He wonders how he will know which hen to choose. There are so many!

Kojo tries to look over *all* the chickens. A white one pecks the ground near his foot. Should he choose this hen? A speckled one flaps her wings and clucks. Perhaps she is the one? All at once Kojo spies a plump brown hen with a bright red comb sitting in her nest and puffing out her feathers. She looks as if she would enjoy laying eggs. Now he doesn't have to think: he knows in his heart that she is the one.

Kojo pays for the brown hen and puts her in a wicker basket. He gently covers the hen with a cloth and lifts the basket onto his head. As he walks home, he dreams about the future and he sees a lot of eggs in it—eggs to eat and, if he is lucky, eggs that he can sell to buy more hens.

That night he puts the basket with the hen beside his bed-mat to keep it safe.

This is the hen that Kojo buys
with the loan he got.

9

Kojo makes a nest for his hen from an old wash-powder box and checks it for eggs every day. On the first day he finds … nothing. On the second, still no – but what is this? In the corner, under some straw, a smooth brown egg! Kojo is lucky, indeed: his hen does seem to enjoy laying eggs. She lays five eggs the first week. Kojo and his mother eat one egg apiece, and he saves the other three for the market on Saturday.

On market day he walks among the stalls of fruit, vegetables, meats, *kente* cloths and calabash bowls. He finds a good place to set down his small basket and call out for customers. Kojo sells two eggs to Ma Achempong and one to Ma Duodu. He clutches his egg money tightly so he won't lose it. He is about to pack up his basket and go home when he finds another

treasure: loose grains and bits of fruit fallen on the ground that can feed his hen.

Slowly, slowly, Kojo's egg money grows. After two months he saves enough to pay his mother back. In four months he has enough to buy another hen. Now Kojo can sell five eggs a week, and he and his mother have more to eat. After six months he buys a third hen, and he and his mother have an egg a day. Kojo is proud of his eggs. And his mother is proud of Kojo. Bit by bit, one small hen is making a big difference.

These are the eggs that Kojo sells from the hen he bought.

One year later Kojo has built up his flock to twenty-five hens. He thinks the sound of chickens clucking and skittering about their enclosure is better than the beating of festival drums. But collecting eggs from so many hens is hard work. His speckled hen tries to hide her eggs. Today he finds one under a cassava plant. And his white hens peck at him when he checks their nests. Then there is his brown hen with the bright red comb – his first and still his favorite. She always seems to have a smooth brown egg for him.

Selling eggs at the market has given Kojo some savings. Maybe he will use his egg money to build a fine wooden chicken coop. Maybe he will buy some things his mother needs, such as a new water bucket and a good knife. Or maybe he can pay for something he's been dreaming of: fees and a uniform so that he can go back to school.

"Your eggs have made us stronger, Kojo," says his mother. "Now go to school and learn ... for both of us."

These are the chickens Kojo buys with the money he got from selling the eggs

13

This is the school Kojo attends with the fees he paid from the money he made selling his eggs.

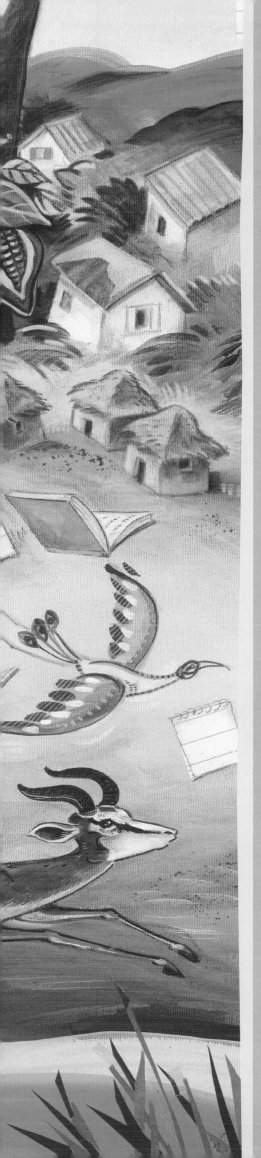

Kojo's uniform feels stiff and new as he walks to school. With each step his lips move silently, reciting the ABCs and numbers he learned before his father died.

In school Kojo works hard to catch up with other students on reading and spelling and arithmetic. Later he learns to write essays and solve math and science problems. And he learns about his country's history and its resources and about other countries in Africa and around the world.

There are practical lessons for country life, too: how to filter drinking water with a cloth to remove parasites; how to use chicken manure and compost made from garbage to fertilize soil and grow vegetables. The lessons Kojo learns help him care for his chickens.

His dreams are growing bigger, but now he sees that he will need more education to make them come true. Kojo studies even harder and wins a scholarship to an agricultural college to learn more about farming. His mother will care for his chickens while he is away.

At college Kojo's dreams start to take shape – the shape of a farm of his own.

After Kojo finishes college, he decides to take a big risk. He will use all the money he and his mother have saved to start a real poultry farm. He buys a large plot of land and enough wood and wire to build chicken coops. Now he needs hens – nine hundred of them – to start the farm. He needs another loan – and a big one.

This time Kojo goes to a bank in Kumasi, a nearby town. When the banker hears that Kojo wants to buy nine hundred hens, he shakes his head. He does not want to lend money to a young man from a poor family.

Kojo does not give up. He goes to the capital city, Accra, and visits the bank's headquarters. Kojo waits and waits to see the bank president. The bank is near closing when, finally, the president agrees to see him. But not for long. He is a busy man.

Kojo tells the banker that he has schooling and will work hard. The banker has heard such stories before and frowns. Then Kojo tells him about the small loan and the brown hen and the egg money he has used to build his flock.

The banker sits back in his chair. He taps his fingers together. This is not a story he hears every day. He smiles and nods – Kojo will get his loan. The banker and Kojo shake hands.

Back home Kojo buys his hens. Soon there will be eggs – so many eggs that he will need helpers to collect them all.

This is the farm that Kojo builds using the lessons he learned at college and a loan from a bank.

This is the family Kojo raises on the farm he built with money he made.

Kojo's hens are good layers. There are more than enough eggs for his village, so he travels to Kumasi to sell to the shopkeepers there.

One shopkeeper is called Kwasi. Kojo knows him well. This man grew up in the same village that Kojo's father did and was his good friend. Kojo always goes to Kwasi's shop last and sometimes stays for supper. He likes to hear stories about his father. And he likes the peanut stew and palm oil soup that Kwasi's daughter makes.

Her name is Amma, and she is a teacher. She has many stories about boys just like Kojo once was—boys who want to learn and who have big dreams. Kojo loves these stories, and he visits more and more often. He wishes he could hear Amma's stories every day. One day he asks if she will be his wife.

Amma is proud to marry Kojo and join him on the farm. Soon Kojo and Amma are to be parents. As the years go by, they have three boys and two girls, all strong and clever. With the money from Kojo's eggs they build a bigger house of cinderblocks and stucco. Kojo's mother comes to live with them and tend the garden. She will never have to sell firewood again.

Before long, many people are working on Kojo's farm. Men come to feed the chickens and clean the coops. Women collect the eggs and pack them in boxes. Still other workers drive the eggs to markets in Kumasi and Accra.

The workers have families. In all, one hundred and twenty people depend on the wages from Kojo's farm. Families like the Odonkors have enough food to eat and money for their children's school fees. Ma Odonkor can buy medicine when her daughter Adika falls ill. Pa Odonkor can rebuild the walls of their mud home with cinderblocks and buy wood-stamped *adinkra* cloths for special occasions.

The workers on Kojo's farm can even afford livestock of their own. Some families buy a goat, others a sheep, and some start with one brown hen.

These are the people Kojo hires to work on the farm he built.

21

This is the town that grows as Kojo sells his eggs and pays his workers.

Kojo's farm is now the largest in Ghana. And his town has grown, too. Some people come to find jobs on the farm and build homes for their families. Others come to the town to open shops and sell wares to the workers.

One day, as Kojo tallies the accounts, he hears a knock at the door. Adika Odonkor, all grown up now, is there. She greets Kojo and then holds out a small sack of coins.

She tells Kojo that she has saved her wages. With just a bit more, she says, she could buy a mechanical grain mill and start a small business helping families turn their grain into flour. Would it be possible to have a small loan?

Kojo knows Adika's family well — they have worked on the farm many years. He likes this idea. But he makes Adika promise that one day she will loan money to another family.

Adika agrees and, bit by bit, as one person helps another, the lives of many families in the town improve, and so do the lives of their children. More children have enough to eat, more children go to school and more children are healthy.

As the years pass, Kojo's poultry farm becomes the largest in all of West Africa. He is older now and a proud grandfather. His grandchildren visit often and help collect eggs. "Where will this one go?" they ask. "And that one?"

"To Bamako in Mali," Kojo replies, "or to Ouagadougou in Burkina Faso." Kojo's workers pack thousands of eggs a day, and Kojo feels proud each time an egg truck pulls away to take food to families in neighboring countries.

By now Kojo has paid many taxes to the government of Ghana. So have his workers and the shopkeepers who sell his eggs. The government uses the tax money to build roads, schools and health clinics across the country. It uses the money to improve the port at Accra where ships from many countries come to trade.

One more egg truck drives away, and Kojo looks down at his youngest grandson. The next time the boy asks Kojo where an egg will go, Kojo will say, "To your future, my child."

AFRICA

Ghana

Mali

Burkina Faso

This is the country that grows as businesses like Kojo's and Adika's prosper.

And it all started with one small loan
to buy one brown hen.

This is the way that one young boy named Kojo, with one small loan to buy one brown hen, eventually changed the lives of his family, his community, his town and his country. It all started with a good idea and a small loan that made it come true. It all started with one hen.

A Real Kojo

*T*his is the story of Kwabena Darko, a real boy from Ghana's Ashanti region who really did lose his father and have to help his mother support his family.

Kwabena was born to poor parents who lived in a small town not far from Kumasi in central Ghana. He lost his father at an early age and had to start selling fruit and vegetables door-to-door to pay for his school fees and help his family. Sometimes Kwabena's family did not know where their next meal would come from.

Kwabena's mother remarried — her new husband received a gift of one hundred chicks from a missionary, and Kwabena raised them and sold their eggs. He won a scholarship to study poultry science at college in Israel and returned to Ghana to hone his farming skills. In 1966, he invested his life savings, less than $1000, in land and chickens. Like Kojo, he needed a loan, and he, too, had a struggle to convince the bank to lend him money.

Kwabena's business began to flourish. As he became successful, he never forgot how important it was to make loans available to people who wanted to start their own businesses, and he knew that banks were nervous about such loans. So he decided to start Sinapi Aba (Mustard Seed) Trust to give out loans. The loans were small, only about $200 each, but they made a big difference. Since its founding, Sinapi Aba Trust has provided services to hundreds of thousands of Ghanaians, mostly loans for small businesses such as selling fruit or firewood, sewing clothes, baking snacks, transporting goods or raising small livestock, like the hen that Kojo bought.

For many years, a loan from Sinapi Aba was made to a group of people. Each member received a small amount of money, used it to make more money and then paid it back. The whole group ensured that the loan was repaid each time. About three quarters of the people who received loans were women like Kojo's mother.

Sinapi Aba became part of the global microfinance network Opportunity International (www.opportunity.org), and Kwabena served on its board of directors. Today, Sinapi Aba is an independent savings and loan company.

"I often tell people that when I was young and struggling, somebody gave me a chance," says Kwabena. "All I want to do now is to be part of something that gives young people the same break I received."

What can you do to help?

Would you like to provide a small loan to a "Kojo"? There are a number of organizations that donate money to "village banks," such as Sinapi Aba's original branches in Ghana, BancoSol in Bolivia and Grameen Bank and BRAC in Bangladesh. These and similar groups in other countries lend people money to start or build a small business and pull themselves out of poverty.

And the movement is growing. Dr. Muhammad Yunus and the micro-lending organization he founded, Grameen Bank, won the Nobel Peace Prize in 2006. Some North American–based organizations, such as Opportunity International, ACCION International, FINCA and Women's World Banking, support or directly manage networks of local lenders. Others, such as Kiva, connect donors via the Internet with people who need loans.

In addition, many international development organizations, such as World Vision, Food for the Hungry, Oxfam and Save the Children, now make microfinance part of their community-building efforts. And some North American banks and credit unions, such as Vancity in Canada, are creating services for the poor.

A common approach is either to help local people form savings clubs like Kojo's mother's or to make loans to a group of people. Each person in the group gets some money, uses it to build a business and then pays it back. The loans rotate through one group and then become available to another group. So if you donate $10 to a microfinance program, your $10 could help more than a hundred families over time. It's rare that families fail to pay back the loans because they know the next family needs a chance, too.

If you would like to help someone like Kojo, you can donate to one of many organizations that provide small loans, or microcredit, to people who want to start or build a business.

For free curriculum to teach the concepts of microfinance to elementary and middle-school students, go to www.onehen.org, a unit of BostonScores.org.

Making changes in the world, one person, one family, one community at a time ...

*H*ere are some other people who are being helped with a small loan from a microcredit organization.

Crisanta Pastidio of the Philippines and her family faced poverty when her husband was laid off work. Crisanta taught him the craft of making brooms from palm trees. With the help of a small loan from a member of the Women's World Banking network (www.swwb.org), they expanded production. With two more loans they've added other goods, such as furniture, cooking wares, household decorations, crafts, native hats and bags.

Emily Syabubila of Zambia is a widow with three children. She received her first loan, the equivalent of $75, along with business training from World Vision's local partner, VisionFund Zambia. She bought a sewing machine and built up a business making school uniforms. With a second loan, she added a fish-trading business, and with a third she went into agriculture, growing vegetables. By 2011, she was on her fifth loan, had expanded her businesses, bought furniture for her home and sent all her children to school.

Gabriela Camacho Diaz of Peru works every day in one of Ventanilla's hot and hectic marketplaces selling fruit. After two years and four loans from a partner of ACCION International (www.accion.org), she has expanded her table into a well-stocked fruit stand with scales and a tarp. "Now, I am not always worried," Gabriela says. "I finally have enough money."

One small loan can make a big difference.

31

Glossary

adinkra cloth: a cloth made by the Ashanti people of Ghana that is worn on special occasions. It is stamped with symbols, each of which has a different meaning.

Ashanti: one of Ghana's major groups of people. They share a common language.

calabash: a big gourd that grows on a vine. It can be eaten as a vegetable or dried and used as a bottle, utensil or pipe.

cassava: also called "manioc," is a potato-like root that is full of starch. It is the main food of many poor people living in tropical climates.

cinderblocks: cement blocks used to build permanent homes. Starter homes are often made of mud and straw or tin siding.

compost: a mixture made from old vegetables, grass cuttings and other organic material that is used to help plants grow

fufu: a main food of West and Central Africa. It is a thick paste or porridge usually made by boiling starchy root vegetables in water and pounding them until they are like mashed potatoes.

kente cloth: a cloth of the Ashanti people in Ghana made of woven fabric strips. It was once worn only for extremely important occasions.

loan: sum of money borrowed from a lender and paid back after a certain period of time

parasites: tiny bugs that live on or in human or animal bodies, often causing illness

profit: money left over after a loan has been repaid

savings: money that is set aside for later

school fees: money paid to a school for attendance and other expenses. In Ghana, children have to buy their school supplies and uniforms. Many families do not have enough money for these fees.

scholarship: money that the government or some other organization or individual gives a student to cover the cost of his or her studies

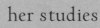